MW00764094

THE VEGETARIAN KETOGENIC DIET COOKBOOK

50 HEALTHY & TASTY VEGETARIAN KETO RECIPES TO HELP EASE YOU INTO A HEALTHIER LIFESTYLE & PROMOTE WEIGHTLOSS.
+BONUS RECIPES

CONTENTS

INTRODUCTION

I want to thank you and congratulate you for downloading this book, "Vegetarian Ketogenic Diet: Healthy & Tasty Vegetarian Keto Recipes to Help Ease You into a Healthier Lifestyle & Mindset".

This book contains basic information about the Ketogenic Diet, but this time, borrowing the principles of the vegetarian diet. The Keto diet is one that advocates eating mostly fats, some lean protein, and very little carbs. This diet suggests daily consumption of 75% fats, 20% protein, and 5% carbs. However, because the keto diet is all meat, and if what consumed is packaged meat such as hotdogs, sausages, bacon, and salami, then you may increase the risk of diabetes and heart diseases.

This is why the vegetarian ketogenic diet was born. This is a meat-free diet that still restricts carbohydrates. By eating this way, you get to enjoy the full benefits of the keto diet by decreasing animal consumption and animal abuse, carbon footprint, and improving one's overall health.

In this cookbook, you are going to learn more about the Keto Vegetarian diet as well as the many recipes that can help you with your meal plan.

Thanks again for downloading the book. I hope you enjoy it!

CHAPTER ONE

THE KETO-VEGETARIAN DIET

This diet mainly includes the use of eggs and dairy. There will be no meat, poultry, and fish. In order to implement this kind of diet to the letter, specific rules must be followed:

- ✓ Carbohydrate intake for a day must only be 35 grams or less

- ✓ Always go for low carb vegetables such as broccoli, asparagus, mushrooms, spinach, zucchini, green beans, bell peppers, cauliflower, and kale among others

- ✓ All animal meat must be completely eliminated from one's diet

While on the ketogenic diet, it is important that you completely avoid sugars like honey, maple syrup, and agave, legumes such as peas, lentils, and black beans, tubers such as potatoes, and grains such as rice, wheat, cereal, and corn. These foods are high in carbohydrates that only one serving of any of these can take you beyond your recommended limit of carbs in a day.

For more keto vegetarian options, stick to vegan meats. By this we mean tempeh, seitan, and tofu among others. Go for above ground veggies such as zucchini, cauliflower, and broccoli. You will also never go wrong adding berries and avocado in your diet. Other dairy products such as butter, hard cheeses, and high fat cream can also be consumed. When it comes to other fats, olive oil, red palm oil, and coconut oil are allowed. For nuts and seeds, go for pumpkin seeds, pistachios, almonds, and sunflower seeds. Finally, for sweeteners, choose stevia, Erythritol, monk fruit, and aspartame among others.

Sticking to the vegetarian keto diet food list, you can be both a vegetarian and keto-er all at the same time. Plus, you get to benefit going plant-based. However, you may be thinking that it would be hard to get enough fat now that you've eliminated fish and meat into your diet. The good news is, there are healthy, vegetarian fats such as olive oil, avocado oil, nuts, seeds, yogurt, cream cheese, and butter among others.

How about protein if meat is not allowed? How should one get enough protein?

Relying on cheeses and eggs alone just won't cut it. Good thing there are other vegetarian protein sources such as:

Tofu – this is high in calcium and protein. This is most vegetarians' tasty alternative for poultry, meat, and fish. Tofu may be a little soft and mushy but you can always buy the firm option, freeze it, and press as much liquid to make it chewier just like the regular meat.

Tempeh – this fermented soy is definitely firmer than tofu, and is a good alternative for beef and fish.

Seitan – this is another meat substitute that is made from soy sauce, wheat gluten, seaweed, garlic, and ginger. However, this contains a lot of gluten, so if you're allergic to gluten, then you might consider other vegetarian protein alternatives.

Nuts and Seeds – some examples with the most protein per 100 grams are almonds, pumpkin seeds, sunflower seeds, pistachios, and flaxseeds.

Protein powder – this can be added to your smoothies and power juices. There are organic and grass-fed whey protein powder available. If you think you're short of protein for the day, try adding protein powder to your smoothie. Of course, you need to choose those low carb smoothies so you won't go beyond our carb limit. You may also choose to add flavorless powder to your meals such as pea protein and whey protein.

Try other replacements such as coconut cream instead of heavy cream, vegan butter instead of butter, vegan soft cheese, instead of cream cheese, and nut based yogurt instead of sour cream and yogurt.

Finally, when buying keto-vegan alternatives, make sure you check the labels for added sugar, hydrogenated oils, and hidden carbs.

For best results, here's a comprehensive list of vegetarian-keto food that you can include in your shopping list:

Shopping List Guide:

- Plant based fats such as red palm oil and olive oil

- Fruits such as avocado, lemons, cantaloupe, melons, berries, and apples

- Vegetables such asparagus, broccoli, Eggplant, Brussels sprout, baby kale, Cucumbers, cabbage, Cauliflower, Tomatoes, Celery, Mushrooms, Garlic, bell pepper, Romaine lettuce, onions and shallots, Scallions, Spinach, Iceberg lettuce, Spaghetti squash, and Zucchini

- Coconut products such as coconut oil, coconut butter, full-fat coconut milk, and unsweetened coconut flakes

- Dairy Products –creams and cheeses such as cheddar, cottage, parmesan, mozzarella, pepper jack, and ricotta cheese. Creams such as sour cream and heavy cream are allowed but should be consumed in moderation.

- Olives and olive oil

- Nuts, nut butters, and seeds such as cashews and cashew butter, peanuts and peanut butter, almonds and almond butter, chia, pumpkin, sunflower seeds, macadamia, pistachio, pecans, and walnuts.

- Sweeteners and extracts such as liquid or granulated stevia, powdered or granulated Erythritol, vanilla extract, orange extract, peppermint, and almond extract.

- Condiments such as hot sauce, apple cider vinegar, and mustard among others

- Dark chocolate

- Cocoa powder, unsweetened

Advantages/Benefits to the Ketogenic Diet

The very foundation of the Ketogenic diet is the breakdown of fatty acids. This process produces ketone bodies that supply energy to different cells in the body. However, ketones not only supply energy, they also deliver many other health benefits.

Ketosis not only aids in the treatment of epilepsy, it also helps in the treatment of other medical conditions such as high cholesterol, type-2 diabetes, and other degenerative diseases. Of course, being in a state of ketosis is also known to be very effective in weight loss.

Ketogenic diet and weight loss

The Ketogenic diet promotes weight loss in the following ways:

1. This diet ensures that there are fewer calories consumed thereby preventing you to gain extra pounds.

2. The Keto diet helps get rid of excess fat in the body. Fat metabolism is greatly increased because the ketone bodies are needed to fill in the energy gap produced by low carb intake. Therefore, stored fats are deployed and burned, including those found in the arms, hips, and tummy area.

3. The ketogenic diet helps in managing one's hunger pangs. And because this diet promotes fatty food, fiber, and protein, starvation is never a problem. One feels fuller for longer period of time. According to studies, eating fatty foods suppress hormones responsible for feeling hungry.

Health Benefits of the Keto Diet

- Helps fight cancer – patients who were suffering from colon, gastric, and prostate cancers that followed a Ketogenic diet showed delayed progression of their disease weigh against those who did not follow the said diet. Although Science has yet to find out the exact reason, some have theorized that the lack of glucose has starved cancer cells where they usually thrive and survive.

- Helps manage blood sugar levels – once you follow the ketogenic diet, the glucose levels tend to normalized and become steady all throughout the day. Because high-sugar and high-carb foods are eliminated or greatly reduced in the Keto diet, insulin sensitivity is likewise improved. This is positive news for people with diabetes and hypertension.

- Brain functioning is enhanced – ketones protect the neurons from degenerating and in overall neurological functioning. This primarily prevents Alzheimer's and Parkinson's diseases. There have also been studies stating that a fat-fueled brain is more advantageous than a glucose-fueled brain.

Chapter Two

Ketogenic-Vegetarian Breakfast Recipes

Recipe #1 – Chilled Almond Soup

Ingredients:

- 3 slices, gluten free bread, remove crust
- 3 cups water, chilled, divided
- 2 garlic cloves, sliced
- 1 cup almonds, blanched
- 5 Tbsp. olive oil
- 5 tsp. sherry vinegar
- Pinch of sea salt
- Pinch of ground black pepper

- flaked almonds, toasted, for garnish
- Grapes, seedless, for garnish

Directions:

1. In a large bowl, break the bread. Pour 2 cups chilled water. Set aside for 5 minutes.
2. Meanwhile, put together garlic and almonds in a blender. Process until the mixture is finely ground. Add in soaked bread. Process until smooth.

3. Gradually pour olive oil until a paste consistency is achieved. Pour sherry vinegar and the remaining chilled water. Season with salt and pepper. Process until smooth.
4. Place mixture inside the fridge for 2 -4 hours.
5. To serve, ladle soup into chilled bowl. Garnish with almonds and grapes.

Recipe #2 - Banana-Walnuts Pancakes

Ingredients:

- 1 banana, mashed
- ½ cup walnuts, toasted, chopped
- 1 tbsp. baking powder
- 1 cup whole wheat flour, finely milled
- ¼ tsp. salt
- 1 cup coconut milk
- 2 tbsp. coconut oil, melted
- 2 tbsp. pure maple syrup
- 1 tsp. vanilla extract

Directions:

1. Mix banana, walnuts, baking powder, whole wheat flour, salt, 1 cup coconut milk, coconut oil, pure maple syrup, vanilla extract in a mixing bowl. Do not over mix.
2. Meanwhile, lightly grease skillet with oil.
3. Divide batter into equal amounts. Pour into the skillet. Cook until the center is runny and the edges set.
4. Plate. Drizzle in maple syrup all over. Serve.

Recipe #3 –Mushroom and Miso Soup

Ingredients:

- 2 Tbsp. coconut oil
- 1 cup sweet onion, diced
- 2 garlic cloves, minced
- ½ cup celery, diced
- ½ cup leek, diced
- 1 Thai red chilli, chopped
- 1 Tbsp. lime juice, freshly squeezed
- 1 Tbsp. miso paste
- ½ Tbsp. cumin
- ½ Tbsp. coriander
- ½ Tbsp. paprika
- Pinch of salt
- Pinch of ground black pepper
- 1 cup enoki mushrooms, halved
- 2 cups oyster mushrooms, diced
- 3 cups vegetable stock
- ½ tsp. Sriracha sauce
- 1 green onion, minced
- ¼ cup bean sprouts

Directions:

1. Pour coconut oil on a stockpot set over medium heat.
2. Once hot, sauté sweet onion, garlic, celery, and, leeks until tender. Add in chili, lime juice, and miso paste. Stir well. Season with cumin, coriander, paprika, salt, and pepper.
3. Tip in enoki and oyster mushrooms. Sauté for 3 minutes or until tender.

4. Pour vegetable stock. Bring to a boil. Once boiling, reduce the heat and allow to simmer for 10 minutes.
5. Add in Sriracha sauce. Cook for 10 minutes. Garnish with green onion and bean sprouts. Serve.

Recipe #4 - Spicy Escarole and Cucumbers Salad

Ingredients:

For the Dressing

- 1 Tbsp. extra-virgin olive oil
- 1 Tbsp. balsamic vinegar
- 1 Tbsp. apple cider vinegar
- 1 Tbsp. lemon juice, freshly squeezed
- ⅛ tsp. sea salt
- Pinch of black pepper
- ½ cup basil leaves, julienned

- 1 escarole, torn
- 1 cup cos lettuce, torn
- 6 cherry tomatoes, quartered
- 1 bird's eye chili, minced
- 2 cucumbers, sliced thinly
- ½ cup black olives in oil, drained

Directions:

1. Whisk olive oil, balsamic vinegar, apple cider vinegar, lemon juice, salt, black pepper, and basil leaves in a bowl. Adjust taste if needed.
2. Place escarole, lettuce, cherry tomatoes, bird's eye chili, cucumbers, black olives in oil in a bowl
3. Drizzle in dressing. Toss gently to combine.
4. To serve, spoon equal amounts into serving plates. Serve.

Recipe #5- Cardamom Pancakes with Dark Chocolate

Ingredients:

- ¼ tsp. cardamom powder
- ½ tsp. baking powder
- ½ tsp. baking soda
- ¼ cup dark chocolate buttons
- 2 Tbsp. maple syrup
- 1 cup all-purpose flour
- 1 cup coconut milk
- 2 tbsp. coconut oil, melted
- 1 tsp. apple cider vinegar
- ¼ tsp. vanilla extract

Directions:

1. Put together cardamom powder, baking powder, baking soda, dark chocolate buttons, maple syrup, all-purpose flour, coconut milk, coconut oil, apple cider vinegar, and vanilla extract in a mixing bowl. Do not over mix.
2. Lightly grease a skillet with oil. Divide batter into equal amounts. Pour into the skillet.
3. Cook until the edges are set and the center bubbly. Do not press down on pancakes.
4. Plate. Sprinkle brown sugar on top. Serve.

Recipe #6 – Apple, Grapes, and Walnuts Salad

Ingredients:

- 2 apples, diced
- 4 green grapes, quartered
- ¼ cup walnuts, roasted, lightly salted

For the Dressing

- 1 tsp. palm sugar, crumbled
- 3 tsp. apple cider vinegar
- Pinch of salt
- Pinch of white pepper
- 1 tsp. extra virgin olive oil

Directions:

1. Place palm sugar, apple cider vinegar, salt, white pepper, and olive oil into a small bottle with tight fitting lid. Shake bottle until salt and sugar dissolve.
2. Place apple, grapes, and walnuts into the bowl. drizzle in dressing. Toss well to combine.
3. To serve, place equal amounts into salad plates.

Recipe #7 – Dates and Blueberries Breakfast Smoothie

Ingredients:

- 2 Medjool dates, chopped
- 1 cup frozen blueberries
- 1 banana, peeled
- 1 cup green tea, chilled
- ¼ tsp. ground cinnamon
- ½ Tbsp. cacao powder
- 1/8 tsp. ground turmeric

Directions:

1. Put together Medjool dates, blueberries, banana, green tea, cinnamon, cacao powder, and ground turmeric in a blender.
2. Cover and blend on high until smooth.

Recipe #8– Banana Pancakes

Ingredients:

- 2 tsp. baking powder
- 1 cup flour
- 1 banana, mashed
- 1 ½ cups soy milk, divided
- 1 tbsp. vegan sweetener such as stevia
- Fruits in season, sliced for garnish

Directions:

1. Sift baking powder and flour in a large bowl.
2. In a separate bowl, add in banana and the pour half the soy milk. Mix. Add in stevia and the remaining milk. Stir until just mixed.
3. Meanwhile, lightly grease a nonstick pan with oil. Pour 1 cup of batter. Cover with a lid. Cook until the edge is set and the center bubbling.
4. Flip pancake over and cook the other side until golden brown.
5. Repeat the same cooking procedure until all batter is cooked. Garnish with fresh fruit of choice. Serve.

Recipe #9 – Macadamia Cheese

Ingredients:

- 1 cup raw macadamia nuts, soaked in water overnight, rinsed, drained, chopped
- 1 tsp. lemon juice, freshly squeezed
- ⅛ tsp. sea salt
- Water, for blending

Directions:

1. Place almonds, salt, and lemon juice into a food processor. Pour just enough water to cover nuts. Pulse until smooth.
2. Drape cheesecloth into fine-meshed colander. Pour mixture to drain. Tie cheesecloth into a knot. Squeeze as much liquid as possible. Place colander into deep dish. Set aside for 24 hours.
3. After 24 hours, discard whey. Transfer to the fridge for 1 hour to set.
4. Remove cheesecloth. Slice cheese according to your preferred shape. Use as needed.

Recipe #10 - Scrambled Spinach Tofu

Ingredients:

- ½ tbsp. olive oil
- 1 yellow onion, minced
- ½ tsp. garlic, minced
- ½ bell pepper, minced
- 8 oz. extra firm tofu
- 1 tbsp. nutritional yeast
- ½ cup spinach
- ¼ tsp. turmeric
- ½ tsp. cumin
- ½ tsp. paprika
- Pinch of sea salt
- Pinch of ground black pepper

Directions:

1. Pour olive oil in skillet. Sauté onion, garlic, and bell pepper for 3 minutes or until tender.
2. Add in crumbled tofu into the skillet. Sauté. Cook spinach spices and nutritional yeast. Season with turmeric, cumin, paprika, salt, and pepper.
3. Sauté until golden and heated through. Serve.

CHAPTER THREE

KETO-VEGETARIAN LUNCH RECIPES

Recipe #11 – Vegetarian Tofu Tacos

Ingredients:

- 2 vegetarian tortillas

- 1 tsp. olive oil
- ½ cup firm tofu, crumbled
- ½ onion, chopped
- 1/8 tsp. dried oregano
- ½ tbsp. chilli power
- ½ tsp. garlic powder
- ½ tbsp. light soy sauce
- 1/8 tsp. cumin

For the Toppings

- 2 tbsp. tomato sauce
- 1 cup lettuce, shredded
- ¼ cup tomato, chopped
- ¼ cup green onion
- 2 ½ tbsp. salsa

Directions:

1. Pour olive oil in a frying pan. Swirl pan to coat.
2. Sauté onion and tofu until the onion is translucent. Add in oregano, garlic powder, soy sauce, chili powder, and cumin. Cook until the tofu is crumbly.
3. Pour tomato sauce. Reduce the heat and allow to simmer until the liquid has evaporated.
4. Meanwhile, reheat tortillas in a nonstick pan. Transfer to a plate.
5. Spoon tofu filling on the heated tortilla. Add in lettuce, green onion, tomato, and salsa. Roll up. Serve immediately.

Recipe #12 - Stir-fried Mushrooms and Bamboo Shoots

Ingredients:

- 1/2 Tbsp. peanut oil
- 1 garlic clove, minced
- 1/4 lb. fresh shiitake mushrooms, stems removed, thinly sliced
- 2 Tbsp. vegetable stock
- 1 lb. bamboo shoots, rinsed, drained
- Pinch of sea salt
- Pinch of ground black pepper

Directions:

1. Pour peanut oil into a wok. Once hot, sauté garlic and shiitake mushrooms and sauté for 2 minutes or until the garlic is fragrant and the mushrooms lightly seared.
2. Pour vegetable stock. Add in bamboo shoots. Stir fry for 2 minutes. Season with salt and pepper to taste.
3. Transfer to a serving dish. Serve immediately.

Recipe #13 - Italian Zucchini Chickpea Pasta

Ingredients:

- 1 bay leaf
- 1 garlic clove
- 1 onion, chopped
- ½ chili pepper, chopped
- ¾ lb. zucchini pasta
- ½ lb. cherry tomatoes, quartered
- 6 oz. canned chickpeas, rinsed, drained thoroughly
- 1 Tbsp. fresh basil leaves, chopped
- 2 tsp. sea salt
- Pinch of ground black pepper, to taste
- Pecorino Romano cheese

Ingredients:

1. Mix garlic, chickpeas, bay leaf, and half of sea salt into a saucepan. Pour just the right amount of water. Cover. Bring mixture to a boil for 5 minutes, or until the chickpeas are tender.
2. Drain the mixture. Discard bay leaf. Set aside.
3. Meanwhile, pour olive oil in a skillet. Once hot, sauté onion until tender. Add in cherry tomatoes, basil, and chili pepper. Season with salt and pepper.
4. Reduce the heat and allow to simmer for 5 minutes.
5. Stir in chickpeas. Mix until all ingredients are well-incorporated. Cover and cook for 5 minutes, or until heated through.
6. For the pasta, place zucchini pasta in a bowl. Pour sauce all over. Garnish with pecorino cheese on top. Serve.

Recipe #14 - Broccoli with Molasses Dressing

Ingredients:

For the Dressing

- 1/4 cup vegetable stock
- 1/4 Tbsp. tamari
- 1/4 Tbsp. xanthan gum
- 1 garlic clove, minced
- Ground ginger
- Dash of crushed red pepper flakes
- 1/4 Tbsp. molasses

- 1/2 tsp sesame oil, toasted
- 3/4 lb. broccoli florets
- 1/4 tsp sea salt
- Pinch of ground black pepper

Directions:

1. To prepare the dressing, pour vegetable stock, tamari, xanthan gum, and garlic in a saucepan. Stir in a dash of ginger and red pepper flakes. Mix well.
2. Reduce the heat and allow to simmer until the sauce thickens. Add in molasses. Season with salt and pepper. Set aside.
3. Meanwhile, in a nonstick skillet, pour water and then boil. Place broccoli florets and then season with the salt.
4. Cover and cook for 3 minutes, or until broccoli is tender.

5. Transfer broccoli to a bowl. Drizzle in sesame oil all over. Season with black pepper. Toss well to coat. Serve right away.

Recipe #15 - Cream of Lentil Soup

Ingredients:

- 1 ½ Tbsp. olive oil
- 1 onion, peeled, diced
- 1 ½ celery sticks, diced
- 1 carrot, peeled, diced
- ¾ cup brown lentils, rinsed
- 3 cups vegetable stock
- Pinch of sea salt
- Pinch of ground black pepper, to taste
- ¾ tsp. ground coriander

Ingredients:

1. Pour olive oil in a saucepan set over medium heat through. Once hot, sauté onion, celery, and carrots until tender. Add in brown lentils. Season with salt, pepper, and coriander.
2. Pour vegetable stock. Stir well. Bring to a boil.
3. Once boiling, reduce heat and allow to simmer for 25 minutes, or until lentils are tender.
4. Let cool before transferring to a blender. Blend. Reheat in a saucepan over low flame.
5. Divide into equal servings. Serve.

Recipe #16 - Baby Veggies Stir Fry on Zucchini Pasta

Ingredients:

- 2 cups zucchini noodles, processed using a spiralizer

For the Sauce

- ¼ tsp. brown sugar
- ½ Tbsp. organic soy sauce
- ½ Tbsp. sunflower oil
- ½ Tbsp. sesame oil
- 1 ½ Tbsp. lime juice, freshly squeezed

- ½ Tbsp. coconut oil
- 1 red onion, peeled, thinly sliced
- 3 baby zucchini, thinly sliced on the diagonal
- 1 cup white cabbage, shredded
- 1 lemongrass stick, peeled, chopped
- 1 red chili pepper, seeded, chopped

Directions:

1. Boil zucchini noodles in a saucepan for 3 minutes. Drain under cold running water to prevent overcooking. Set aside.
2. Meanwhile, mix brown sugar, soy sauce, sunflower oil, sesame oil, and lime juice in a bowl. Set aside.
3. Pour coconut oil in a wok. Once hot, sauté lemongrass and chili pepper, or until fragrant.
4. Add in red onion, baby corn, baby zucchini, and white cabbage. Cook until crisp tender. Pour sauce all over.

5. Reduce the heat and allow to simmer until the liquids are almost completely gone. Stir fry until crisp.
6. Place zucchini noodles on a platter. Add stir fried veggies on top. Serve immediately.

Recipe #17 - Cream of Broccoli Soup

Ingredients:

- 1 onion, chopped
- 1 russet potato, peeled diced
- 3 cups broccoli florets
- ½ cup almond milk, unsweetened
- 1 Tbsp. olive oil
- 1 Tbsp. whole wheat flour
- Pinch of sea salt, to taste

Directions:

1. Put together onion, broccoli, and potato, in a soup pot set over low heat. Pour vegetable stock. Cover and cook for 30 minutes, or until tender.
2. Mash solids using a potato masher or you can also transfer to an immersion blender. Puree until smooth. Set aside.
3. Meanwhile, pour olive oil in a saucepan. Once heated, add in whole wheat flour to make a roux. Pour almond milk. Mix until well-incorporated.
4. Stir in milk mixture into the soup. Season with salt.
5. To serve, ladle soup into bowls. Serve.

Recipe #18 - Lemon Garlic Broccoli

Ingredients:

- 1 broccoli head, chopped into bite-sized florets
- 1 ½ tbsp. olive oil
- 1 garlic clove, minced
- Pinch of sea salt
- Pinch of black pepper to taste
- ¼ tsp. lemon juice, freshly squeezed

Directions:

1. Preheat the oven to 400 degrees F.
2. Spread broccoli and garlic clove on a baking sheet. Drizzle in olive oil all over florets. Season with salt and pepper. Squeeze in lemon juice. Toss well to coat.
3. Place inside the oven and roast for 15 minutes. Serve warm.

Recipe #19 - Roasted Fennel

Ingredients:

- 2 fennel bulbs, sliced off top ends, sliced into half-inch pieces
- Pinch of sea salt
- Pinch of ground black pepper
- 1/4 cup olive oil
- 2 lemons, halved

Directions:

1. Preheat the oven to 375 degrees F. Coat a rimmed baking sheet with olive oil. Set aside.
2. Spread out fennel on the prepared baking sheet. Drizzle in olive oil. Season with salt and pepper, toss well to coat.
3. Place inside the oven and roast for 20 minutes.
4. Turn over fennel, and then roast again for another 20 minutes.
5. Remove from the baking sheet. Let cool on a cooling rack. Squeeze in lemon juice all over. Serve immediately.

Recipe #20 - Roasted Pepper and Sweet Potato Soup

Ingredients:

- 2 tbsp. olive oil
- 2 red peppers
- 1 sweet potato, cubed
- ½ cup onion, chopped
- 2 garlic cloves, minced
- ½ cup carrots, chopped
- ½ cup celery, chopped
- 2 cups vegetable broth
- ½ cup coconut milk
- ¼ cup sweet basil, julienned
- Pinch of sea salt
- Pinch of ground pepper

Directions:

1. Preheat the oven to the 375 degrees F.
2. Meanwhile, mix onions, red peppers, and sweet potatoes on a baking sheet. Drizzle in olive oil all over. Toss well to coat.
3. Place inside the oven and roast for 20 minutes, or until peppers skins are wilted and sweet potatoes are golden. Chop roasted red peppers. Set aside.
4. Pour olive oil in a pot. Once hot, sauté garlic, carrot, and celery until tender. Add roasted red peppers and sweet potato-onion mix.
5. Pour vegetable stock and coconut milk. Season with salt and pepper. Bring to a boil. Once boiling, reduce the heat and allow to simmer for 10 minutes.
6. Turn off the heat. Allow to cool. Add in basil. Mix well. Serve immediately.

CHAPTER FOUR

KETO-VEGETARIAN SNACK RECIPES

Recipe #21 - Squash Flower Pizza

Ingredients

- ½ piece Sourdough Pizza dough

For the toppings

- 6 asparagus spears, sliced into long slivers, rinsed
- ¼ tsp. garlic salt, vegan-safe
- 1 tsp. capers in brine
- 1 can button mushrooms, pieces and stems
- ¼ cup cashew cheese
- 12 squash flowers, petals only, torn
- Pinch of black pepper, to taste
- Extra virgin oil, for drizzling

Directions:

1. Preheat the oven to 430°F. Lightly grease a pizza tray with olive oil.
2. Put the dough on the dough on pizza tray. Stretch dough using your fingers and hands. Season garlic salt.
3. Layer asparagus slivers, capers, and button mushrooms. Put a spoonful of cashew cheese.

4. Spread squash flowers. Season with black pepper and drizzle in olive oil.

5. Place inside the oven and bake for 10 minutes, or until the crust is crisp and flowers turn into brown.

6. Remove pizza tray from the oven. Allow to cool in a cooling rack before slicing.

7. Slice into generous portions slices. Serve warm.

Recipe #22 – Vegan Brownies in Mugs

Ingredients:

- 4 Tbsp. cocoa powder, unsweetened
- ½ cup all-purpose flour
- ½ tsp. baking powder
- 2 Tbsp. liquid stevia
- ½ cup almond milk
- 2 Tbsp. coconut milk
- 4 Tbsp. coconut oil
- ¼ tsp. salt

For garnish

- ½ cup cashew nuts, roasted, unseasoned, halved
- 4 Tbsp. hazelnut chocolate spread, vegan-safe

Directions:

1. Place cocoa powder, all-purpose flour, baking powder, liquid stevia, almond milk, coconut milk, coconut oil, and salt in a mixing bowl. Whisk until lumps disappear.
2. Divide batter into equal amounts. Pour into large mugs. Make sure there is enough room for the cake to rise.
3. Place each mug in the microwave oven. Heat for 1 minute and 15 seconds on high.
4. Carefully remove cake from the oven. Repeat the same cooking procedure as with the rest of the cake mugs.
5. To serve, garnish with cashew nuts and hazelnut chocolate spread in the center.

Recipe #23 - Sweet Potato Hash

Ingredients:

- Olive oil, for greasing
- 1 1/4 tsp dried rosemary
- 4 sweet potatoes, diced
- 2 apples, cored, diced
- Pinch of sea salt
- Pinch of ground black pepper

Directions:

1. Preheat the oven to 400 degrees F. Lightly grease a baking sheet with olive oil. Set aside.
2. Grind rosemary using a mortar and pestle until coarsely ground. Set aside.
3. On the baking sheet, layer apples and sweet potatoes. Season with salt, pepper, and ground rosemary. Toss well to coat.
4. Place inside the oven and bake for 25 minutes, or until golden brown. Serve.

Recipe #24 - Avocado Mango Salad

Ingredients:

- 1 1/2 Tbsp. stevia
- 4 Tbsp. lime juice, freshly squeezed
- Pinch of sea salt
- Pinch of ground white pepper
- 2 ripe avocados, halved, flesh scooped out, sliced into cubes
- 2 red onions, diced
- 2 Tbsp. fresh mint, chopped
- 2 cups fresh cilantro, chopped
- 2 ripe mangoes, diced
- 1/2 cup cashews, roasted, chopped

Directions:

1. Put together stevia, lime juice, salt, and white pepper in a bowl.
2. Add in cubed avocadoes. Toss gently to coat.
3. Stir in red onion, mint, cilantro, mango, and cashews. Toss well to combine.
4. To serve, divide into right amount of servings.

Recipe #25 - Pan-Roasted Chickpeas

Ingredients:

- 2 quarts' water
- ½ lb. fresh chickpeas in the pod
- 2 ½ Tbsp. lemon juice, freshly squeezed
- 2 Tbsp. sea salt
- Extra virgin olive oil, to taste

Directions:

1. Pour water into a pot. Add in salt. Cover and bring to a boil.
2. Add in chickpeas. Blanch for 2 minutes, or until the chickpeas are tender. Drain on paper towels.
3. Pour olive oil in a nonstick skillet. Once hot, add in chickpeas. Cook for 3 minutes, or until browned.
4. Sprinkle lemon juice over chickpeas. Toss well to coat. Transfer to a bowl. Drizzle in olive oil. Season with salt. Serve right immediately.

Recipe #26 - Daikon and Carrot Pickles

Ingredients:

- 1 Tbsp. liquid stevia
- ¼ cup sea salt
- 4 cups non-chlorinated water
- 1 lb. carrots. julienned
- 1 lb. daikon radishes, julienned

Directions:

1. Place stevia and salt into the water until thoroughly dissolved. Set aside.
2. Place carrots and radishes into a clean jar. Pour enough brine to cover them. Make sure vegetables are completely submerged.
3. Cover the jar with a cheesecloth. Secure with rubber bands. Transfer to a cool, dry place. Let it ferment for 7 to 14 days.
4. After 7 days, start taste testing the pickles. Once sour enough, cover the lid and transfer to the refrigerator. This can keep in the fridge for 1 year.

Recipe #27- Celery Relish

Ingredients:

- ¾ lb. celery stalk and leaves, chopped finely
- 5 fresh sage leaves, chopped finely
- ½ Tbsp. fresh thyme, chopped
- ½ tsp sea salt

Directions:

1. Place chopped celery, sage, and thyme in a bowl. Sprinkle salt all over. Massage everything until the vegetables start to sweat. Cover and set aside for 30 minutes.
2. Once the celery has released a good amount of brine, transfer everything into a clean jar. Press down on the celery mixture to ensure it is submerged in the brine. You can use a sheet of food-grade plastic wrap or other type of weight to keep the solids submerged.
3. Cover the jar with a cheesecloth. Secure with rubber bands. Transfer to a cool, dry place. Let it ferment for 5 to 10 days.
4. After 5 days, start taste testing the celery relish. Once sour enough, you can transfer to small jars. Cover with the lid. This can keep fresh in the fridge for 10 months.

Recipe #28 - Zucchini Chips

Ingredients:

- 2 zucchinis, sliced into thick disks
- Pinch of sea salt
- Olive oil, for drizzling
- Pinch of black pepper, to taste
- Dash of cayenne powder

Directions:

1. Preheat oven to 250°F/120°C. Line a baking sheet with parchment paper.
2. Season zucchini with salt. Drain for 30 minutes.
3. Remove excess moisture from the vegetables using paper towels.
4. Layer on the baking sheet. Drizzle in olive oil. Season with cayenne powder and black pepper.
5. Place inside the oven and bake for 45 minutes, flipping once.
6. Remove from the oven. Transfer to a cooling rack. Serve.

Recipe #29 - Fried Green Tomatoes

Ingredients:

- 1 lb. fresh green tomatoes, sliced into thick pieces
- 1 cup almond flour, finely milled
- Pinch of salt
- Coconut oil

Directions:

1. Pour coconut oil into a non-stick skillet.
2. Season tomatoes with salt. Dredge tomato slices into the almond flour. Drop into hot oil one by one. Fry until golden brown.
3. Drain on paper towels. Continue cooking until all tomatoes are cooked. Serve.

Recipe #30 - Kale Chips

Ingredients:

- 1 lb. kale leaves, torn
- Pinch of sea salt, to taste
- Melted coconut oil, for drizzling

Directions:

2. Preheat the oven to 300°F. Line a baking sheet with parchment paper.
3. Place kale leaves into a bowl. Drizzle in coconut oil. Toss well to combine.
4. Spread leaves flatly on the baking sheet. Season with salt. Drizzle in more oil.
5. Place inside the oven and bake for 20 minutes.
6. Remove from the oven. Serve.

Recipe #31 - Spicy Hummus Bruschetta

Ingredients:

- 1 slice focaccia, lightly toasted
- 1½ tbsp. spicy hummus

For toppings

- ½ Tbsp. tomato, diced
- ¼ Tbsp. chives, minced
- ½ Tbsp. cucumber, diced
- ½ Tbsp. pomegranate seeds
- Pinch of salt
- Pinch of white pepper

Directions:

1. Spread spicy hummus on bread.
2. Place inside the oven toaster and heat until warmed through.
3. Meanwhile, put together tomato, chives, cucumber, and pomegranate seeds in a bowl. Season with salt and white pepper.
4. Spread on top of bruschetta. Serve.

CHAPTER FIVE

KETO-VEGETARIAN DINNER RECIPES

Recipe #32 - Vegetarian Sloppy Joes

Ingredients:

- 1 cup plain tempeh, crumbled
- ½ cup barbecue sauce
- ½ tsp. olive oil
- ½ onion, minced
- ½ green bell pepper, minced
- 2 Kaiser rolls, halved

Directions:

1. Place crumbled tempeh in a bowl. Add in barbecue sauce. Set aside for 10-15 minutes to marinate.
2. Meanwhile, pour olive oil in a skillet. Sauté onion and green bell pepper for 3 minutes or until tender.
3. Stir in tempeh with the barbecue sauce. Cook for 2 minutes or until heated through.

Recipe #33 – Apples, Carrots, and Almond Soup

Ingredients:

- 3 red apples, quartered
- 1 white onion, quartered
- 4 carrots, chopped
- 3 cups vegetable stock, unsalted
- 2 tsp. garam masala
- Dash of cinnamon powder
- ⅛ tsp. all spice powder
- Dash of paprika powder
- Pinch of sea salt
- Pinch of black pepper, to taste
- ½ cup Greek yogurt
- 2 Tbsp. almond slivers, toasted
- ¼ tsp. fresh chives, minced, for garnish

Directions:

1. Place apples, onion, carrots, vegetable stock, garam masala, cinnamon powder, all spice powder, paprika powder, salt, and black pepper into the slow cooker.
2. Secure the lid and lock in place. Cook for 8 hours on low.
3. After 8 hours, let the mixture cool before transferring to a food processor.
4. Pour along with the rest of the ingredients. Process until smooth. Adjust taste, if needed.
5. Pour mixture into a freezer-safe container. Place inside the fridge to chill for 1 hour before serving.
6. To serve, pour chilled soup into bowls. Garnish with chives.

Recipe #34 - Strawberry and Grapefruit Salad

Ingredients:

For the dressing
- 1 fresh strawberry, mashed
- 1 tsp. grapefruit juice, freshly squeezed
- ½ tsp. Dijon mustard
- 1 tsp. apple cider vinegar
- 2 Tbsp. extra virgin olive oil
- ¼ tsp. raw, unprocessed honey
- Pinch of sea salt
- Pinch of black pepper, to taste

- 1 head iceberg lettuce, cored, chopped to bite-sized pieces
- ¼ cup baby beet greens, torn
- ½ fresh grapefruit, only the pulp, shredded
- 4 fresh strawberries, quartered
- ½ Tbsp. raw, almond slivers, toasted

Directions:
1. For the dressing, pour strawberry, grapefruit juice, Dijon mustard, apple cider vinegar, olive oil, honey, salt, and black pepper in a bottle with tight fitting lid. Seal. Shake well.
2. For the salad, place iceberg lettuce, baby beet greens, grapefruit, and strawberries in a salad bowl. Toss well to combine.
3. Drizzle in half of the dressing. Toss to coat.

4. Ladle equal amounts of salad on plates. Drizzle in the remaining dressing all over. Scatter almond slivers on top. Serve.

Recipe #35 - Stir-Fried Mushrooms with Peas

Ingredients:

- ½ tsp. coconut oil
- 1 onion, minced
- 1 garlic clove, minced
- ½ cup peas, drained
- 1 can canned button mushrooms, rinsed, drained
- 1 cup vegetable stock
- Pinch of sea salt
- Pinch of white pepper, to taste

Directions:

1. Pour coconut oil in a wok. Sauté onions and garlic for 2 minutes or until limp and fragrant.
2. Add in peas, button mushrooms, and vegetable stock. Season with salt and pepper. Bring mixture to a boil.
3. Turn off the heat. Allow to simmer for 5 minutes. Adjust taste, if needed.
4. Ladle equal amounts into bowls. Serve.

Recipe #36 - Chop Suey

Ingredients:

- 1 tsp. coconut oil
- 2 garlic cloves, minced
- 1 shallot, minced
- 1 cauliflower, slice into florets
- 1 carrot, sliced into florets
- 1 cup vegetable stock
- ¼ red bell pepper, diced
- ¼ cabbage, chopped
- Pinch of sea salt
- Pinch of white pepper, to taste

For garnish

- 1 tsp. fresh cilantro, minced

Directions:

1. Pour coconut oil in a wok. Sauté Add garlic and shallot for 2 minutes or until limp and transparent.
2. Add in carrot and cauliflower. Pour vegetable stock. Allow to simmer for 20 minutes or until the veggies are just tender.
3. Stir in red bell pepper and cabbage. Mix until all ingredients are well-combined. Turn off the heat. Taste. Adjust seasoning, if needed.
4. Ladle equal amounts of chop suey into bowls. Garnish with cilantro.

Recipe #37 - Spinach Avocado Soup

Ingredients:

- 2 garlic cloves, chopped
- ½ lb. fresh spinach, leaves and tender stems
- 1 cup vegetable stock
- Pinch of sea salt
- Pinch of black pepper, to taste
- 1 ripe avocado, flesh scooped out

Directions:

1. Place garlic cloves, spinach, and vegetable stock into a stock pot. Season with salt and black pepper. Bring mixture to a boil.
2. Turn off the heat. Let cool before transferring to a blender.
3. Put avocado flesh along with the mixture. Process until smooth.
4. To serve, pour equal amounts into bowl. Serve.

Recipe #38 - Greens with Salsa Dressing

Ingredients:

For the dressing

- 1 shallot, minced
- 1 garlic clove, grated
- ⅛ tsp. dried pepper flakes
- ½ tsp. English mustard
- ¼ cup extra virgin olive oil
- 2 Tbsp. lemon juice, freshly squeezed
- Pinch of sea salt
- Pinch of black pepper, to taste

- 1 head iceberg lettuce, torn
- 1 green/unripe tomato, julienned
- 1 red/ripe tomato, deseeded, julienned
- 2 sprigs cilantro, minced
- 1 head endive, torn

Directions:

1. For the dressing, put together shallot, garlic clove, dried pepper flakes, English mustard, olive oil, lemon juice, salt, and black pepper into a small bottle with tight fitting lid. Shake well.
2. For the salad, place iceberg lettuce, green and red tomatoes, cilantro, and endive in a salad bowl. Toss well to combine.
3. Drizzle in half of dressing. Toss again to coat.
4. Ladle salad on plates. Drizzle in remaining dressing all over. Serve.

Recipe #39 - Fruit Stew with Cashew Nuts

Ingredients:

- 1 tsp. olive oil
- 1 sweet potato, cubed
- 1 green apple, cubed
- ¼ cup cranberries
- 2 fresh leeks, minced
- 1 celery rib, chopped
- ⅛ tsp. dried thyme
- ⅛ tsp. nutmeg powder
- ¼ cup apple cider vinegar
- 2 cups vegetable stock, unsalted
- Pinch of sea salt
- Pinch of black pepper, to taste

For garnish, all optional

- ½ tsp. fresh cilantro, minced
- 2 Tbsp. raw cashew nuts, chopped, toasted

Directions:

1. Pour olive oil into a Dutch oven. Add in sweet potato, green apple, cranberries, leeks, celery, dried thyme, nutmeg powder, apple cider vinegar, and vegetable stock. Season with salt and pepper.
2. Seal the lid. Bring mixture to a boil. Once boiling, reduce the heat and allow to simmer for 30 minutes.
3. To serve, ladle equal amounts of stew into bowls. Garnish with cilantro and cashew nuts on top.

Recipe #40 - Cauli Mac 'n' Cheese

Ingredients:

- 1 cauliflower head, chopped into bite-sized florets
- ½ cup heavy cream
- ½ cup Cheddar cheese, shredded
- ¼ cup mozzarella cheese, shredded
- ¼ cup Parmesan cheese, shredded
- ¼ cup cream cheese, cubed
- ½ tsp. sea salt
- ¼ tsp. garlic, minced
- 1/8 tsp. ground black pepper
- Nonstick cooking spray

Directions:

1. Preheat the oven to 400 degrees F.
2. Pour just the right amount of water into a pot, covered. Set on high heat. Bring to a boil, Sprinkle some salt.
3. Add in cauliflower florets to the boiling water. Let it boil for 3 minutes. Drain on paper towels. Transfer to a platter. Set aside.
4. Meanwhile, pour heavy cream into the skillet. Allow to simmer whilst stirring continuously. Stir in cream cheese until smooth.
5. Add in garlic, Cheddar cheese, and mozzarella cheese. Cook until cheeses have melted.
6. Turn off the heat. Mix cauliflower into the cheese mixture. Toss well to coat. Season with salt and pepper.
7. Lightly grease a baking dish with nonstick cooking spray. Add in cauliflower and cheese mixture. Scatter Parmesan cheese on top.

8. Place inside the oven and bake for 15 minutes, or until golden brown.
9. Allow to cool slightly before serving.

Recipe #41: Stuffed Portobello Mushrooms with Spinach and Cheeses

Ingredients:

- 6 Portobello mushroom caps, discard gills and stems
- Pinch of sea salt, to taste
- Pinch of ground black pepper, to taste
- 3 garlic cloves, minced
- ¾ cup spinach, steamed
- 2 eggs
- ¾ cup Parmesan cheese, grated
- 1 ¼ cups ricotta cheese
- ½ cup extra virgin olive oil

Directions:

1. Preheat the oven to 425 degrees F. Line a baking sheet with aluminum foil. Set aside.
2. Season the inside of the Portobello caps with salt and pepper. Layer on a baking sheet.
3. Place inside the oven and bake for 15 minutes.
4. Meanwhile, put together garlic cloves, spinach, eggs, Parmesan cheese, ricotta cheese, and olive oil in a bowl. Mix until completely combined. Set aside.
5. Remove mushroom caps out of the oven. Divide filling among them. Return to the oven. Bake for another 25 minutes.
6. Place stuffed mushroom caps on a cooling rack before serving.

CHAPTER SIX

KETO-VEGETARIAN DESSERT AND SMOOTHIES AND TEA RECIPES

Recipe #42 - Sweetened Macadamia Nuts + Cranberry Lime Infusion

Ingredients:

- ¼ cup shelled macadamia nuts, sliced into thick medallions, toasted
- Pinch of sea salt
- ⅛ tsp. liquid stevia

Directions:

1. Place macadamia nuts, salt, and stevia in a bowl. Toss to combine. Serve.

Cranberry Lime Infusion

Ingredients:

- 1 cup frozen cranberries
- 1 lime, quartered
- ¼ tsp. liquid stevia
- 2 cups boiled water

Directions:

2. Place cranberries, lime, and water in a tea infuser.
3. Allow to steep for 5 minutes. Strain.
4. Stir in liquid stevia into individual cups.

Recipe #43 – Fruit Muffins + Black Tea Infusion with Strawberries

Ingredients:

- 3 tsp. baking powder
- 2 cups flour
- 1 ½ cups seasoned fruit of choice
- 2 eggs
- ½ tsp. salt
- ½ cup vegan sweetener of choice
- ¾ cup sour soy milk (add 1 tsp vinegar)
- ¼ cup oil

Directions:

1. Preheat the oven to 350 degrees F.
2. Mix baking powder, flour, seasoned fruit of choice, eggs, salt, vegan sweetener, sour soy milk, and oil in a bowl. Mix well.
3. Scoop mixture into muffin tins. Place inside the oven and bake for 30 minutes. Let cool before serving.

Black Tea Infusion with Strawberries

Ingredients:

- 1 tea bag black tea
- 2 strawberries, sliced thinly
- 2 basil leaves, julienned
- 2½ cups boiled water
- ¼ tsp. liquid stevia, optional

Directions:

1. Place black tea bag, strawberries, basil leaves, and water in a tea infuser.
2. Let steep for 5 minutes.
3. Strain tea. Stir in stevia, if using. Serve.

Recipe #44 – Vegan Coconut Pie + Pineapple Raspberry Infusion

Ingredients:

- 2 cups soft tofu
- ½ cup oil
- ½ tsp. salt
- 1 ½ cups dry sweetener, vegan safe
- 2 tsp. vanilla extract
- 2 1/2 cups coconut, shredded, divided
- 1 graham cracker, pie crust

Directions:

1. Preheat the oven to 350 degrees F.
2. Put together soft tofu, oil, salt, dry sweetener, and vanilla extract in a blender. Blend until smooth.
3. Place graham cracker and 2 cups coconut. Put inside the oven and bake for 15 minutes.
4. Scatter remaining shredded coconut on top. Bake for another 10 minutes. Place inside the fridge for 30 minutes to 1 hour before serving. Serve chilled.

Pineapple Raspberry Infusion

Ingredients:

- 1 cup canned pineapple tidbits
- ½ cup fresh raspberries
- 2 cups boiled water
- ¼ tsp. liquid stevia, optional

Directions:

1. Place pineapple tidbits, raspberries, and boiled water in a tea infuser.
2. Let steep for 5 minutes.
3. Strain tea. Stir in stevia, if using. Serve.

Recipe #45 - Keto Choco Brownies + Grapefruit and Blood Orange Smoothie

Ingredients:

- ¾ Tbsp. baking powder
- 1 scoop whey protein powder, chocolate flavored
- ¾ cup almond flour
- 1/3 cup coconut flour
- ¾ cup cocoa powder, unsweetened
- 3 Tbsp. butter, unsalted
- 6 oz. dark chocolate, 80 percent
- 1/3 cup heavy cream
- 1/3 cup cold water
- 1 ½ tsp. pure vanilla extract
- 3 eggs, beaten

Directions:

1. Preheat the oven to 325 degrees F. Line a square baking pan with baking paper. Set aside.
2. Meanwhile, combine baking powder, whey protein powder, and almond and coconut flours in a bowl. Set aside.
3. Mix cocoa powder, butter, chocolate, heavy cream, and water in another bowl. Place over a pot of simmering water. Mix until combined and melted. Set aside.
4. Add in pure vanilla extract. mix. Whisk in eggs. Mix again.
5. Gradually pour the flour mixture into the chocolate mixture. Transfer to the baking pan.
6. Place inside the oven and bake for 20 minutes. Place on a cooling rack. Let cool for 15 minutes.
7. Slice into equal squares. Serve.

Grapefruit and Blood Orange Smoothie

Ingredients:

- 1 grapefruit, only the pulp
- 1 blood orange, only the pulp
- ½ cup cranberries
- ½ cup crushed ice
- ½ tsp. liquid stevia, optional

Directions:

1. Place grapefruit pulp, blood orange pulp, cranberries, and crushed ice in a blender. Process until smooth.
2. Divide into equal portions. Serve.

Recipe #46 - Cocoa Bites with Cream Cheese + Pineapple Infusion

Ingredients:

- 2 eggs
- 4 oz. butter, melted
- 2 oz. full fat cream cheese
- 1 oz. coconut flour
- ½ tsp. baking soda
- ½ tsp. baking powder
- ½ tsp. xanthan gum
- ½ tsp. pure vanilla extract
- ¼ tsp. liquid stevia

Directions:

1. Preheat the oven to 350 degrees F. Line a rimmed baking sheet with baking paper. Set aside.
2. Whisk butter and cream cheese in a bowl until smooth. Set aside.
3. Put together baking powder, baking soda, coconut flour, and xanthan gum in another bowl. Set aside.
4. In a separate bowl, mix egg, vanilla extract, and liquid stevia. Beat well until smooth.
5. Gradually pour flour mixture into the cream cheese mixture. Add in egg mixture. Mix well.
6. Scoop mixture onto the baking sheet. Place inside the oven and bake for 10 minutes, or until the edges are golden brown.
7. Allow to cool in the cooling rack. Serve.

Pineapple Infusion

Ingredients:

- 1 cup canned pineapple tidbits
- 1 apple, chopped
- 2 cups boiled water
- ¼ tsp. liquid stevia optional

Directions:

1. Place pineapple tidbits, apple, and boiled water in a tea infuser.
2. Let steep for 5 minutes.
3. Strain tea. Stir in stevia, if using. Serve.

Recipe #47 - Poppy Lemon Cupcakes + Apple and Pear Infusion

Ingredients:

- 7 eggs
- 4 oz. butter, melted
- 1 tsp. liquid stevia
- 10 oz. plain Greek yogurt
- 3 oz. coconut flour
- 2 tsp. baking powder
- 2 ½ tsp. lemon zest, grated
- 2 ½ Tbsp. lemon juice, freshly squeezed
- 2 Tbsp. poppy seeds

Directions:

1. Preheat the oven to 375 degrees F. Line cupcake tins with paper liners. Set aside.
2. Meanwhile, whisk eggs, melted butter, liquid stevia, and yogurt in a bowl. Mix. Set aside.
3. In another bowl, mix coconut flour and baking powder. Mix into the egg mixture. Stir until smooth.
4. Stir in zest and lemon juice into the batter. Tip in poppy seeds. Stir until all ingredients are well-incorporated.
5. Pour batter into the cupcake tins. Place inside the oven and bake for up to 30 minutes, or until a toothpick inserted comes out clean.
6. Transfer cupcakes on a cooling rack to cool. Serve.

Apple and Pear Infusion

Ingredients:

- 1 pear, chopped
- 1 apple, chopped
- 2 cups boiled water
- ¼ tsp. liquid stevia, optional

Directions:

1. Place pear, apple, and boiled water in a tea infuser.
2. Let steep for 5 minutes.
3. Strain tea. Stir in stevia, if using. Serve.

Recipe #48 - Carrots Cashew Muffins + Black Tea Infused with Ginger, Lemon, and Basil

Ingredients:

- 4 eggs
- ½ cup steel-cut oats
- 4 carrots, grated
- 2 tsp. baking soda
- 1½ cups whole wheat pastry flour
- ¼ cup cashew nuts, chopped
- 2 tsp liquid stevia
- ¼ cup coconut oil
- 1 tsp. vanilla extract

Directions:

1. Preheat the oven to 375°F. Place paper liners into muffin tins.
2. Meanwhile, put together eggs, oats, carrots, baking soda, whole wheat pastry flour, cashew nuts, liquid stevia, coconut oil, and vanilla extract in a mixing bowl. Do not over mix.
3. Spoon equal portions of batter into paper lined muffin depressions. Place inside the oven and bake for 20 minutes.
4. Remove from the oven immediately.
5. Allow to cool before removing muffins from the tins. Place on cake rack to cool. Serve.

Black Tea Infused with Ginger, Lemon, and Basil

Ingredients:

- 1 tea bag black tea
- 1 fresh ginger, crushed
- ½ lemon, sliced into wedges
- 2 basil leaves, julienned
- 2½ cups boiled water
- ¼ tsp. liquid stevia, optional

Directions:

1. Place black tea bag, ginger, lemon, basil, and boiled water in a tea infuser.
2. Let steep for 5 minutes.
3. Strain tea. Stir in stevia, if using. Serve.

Recipe #49 - Raspberry Cream Cheese Pops + Red Currant and Lime Infusion

Ingredients:

- 4 Tbsp. butter
- ¼ cup cream cheese
- 4 Tbsp. coconut oil
- 4 Tbsp. heavy cream
- ¼ cup fresh raspberries, chopped
- 1 tsp. pure vanilla extract

Directions:

1. Combine butter, cream cheese, and coconut oil in a bowl.
2. Place inside the microwave oven and heat 3 times for 10 seconds interval.
3. Remove bowl from the microwave oven. Stir mixture well. Add in heavy cream and raspberries.
4. Put vanilla extract into the mixture. Mix until all ingredients are well-incorporated.
5. Pour mixture into an ice cube tray. Freeze for 2 hours. Serve chilled.

Red Currant and Lime Infusion

Ingredients:

- 1 cup fresh red currants
- 1 lime, quartered, pips removed
- 2 cups boiled water
- ¼ tsp. liquid stevia, optional

Directions:

1. Place red currants, lime, and water in a tea infuser.
2. Let steep for 5 minutes.
3. Strain tea. Stir in stevia, if using. Serve.

Recipe #50 - Chia Vanilla Granola + Apple Cinnamon Infusio

Ingredients:

- 1/3 cup whey protein powder
- 1 cup macadamia nuts
- ¼ cup water
- 4 Tbsp. flaxseed meal
- 4 Tbsp. whole chia see ds
- 4 Tbsp. coconut oil, melted
- 3 Tbsp. water
- 4 tsp. stevia
- 2 tsp. cinnamon
- 1 tsp. pure vanilla extract
- ¼ tsp. sea salt

Directions:

1. Preheat the oven to 350 degrees F. Line a baking sheet with baking paper. Set aside.
2. Combine chia seeds, vanilla extract, and water in a bowl. Set aside until it becomes gelatinous.
3. Pour macadamia nuts into the food processor. Stir in protein powder, flaxseed meal, cinnamon, stevia, and salt. Pulse until fine and grounded.
4. Pour chia gelatin into the food processor. Pour 1 ½ tablespoons water and coconut oil. Blend until smooth. Set aside.
5. Transfer mixture onto the baking sheet. Place inside the oven and bake for 15 minutes.
6. Remove from the oven. Break into small pieces. Spread out on the pan.

7. Place back in the oven and bake for another10 minutes, or until golden brown. Place on a cooling rack to cool. Serve.

Apple Cinnamon Infusion

Ingredients:

- 1 apple, chopped
- 1 dried cinnamon bark
- 2 cups boiled water
- ¼ tsp. liquid stevia, optional

Directions:

1. Place apple, dried cinnamon bark, and boiled water in a tea infuser.
2. Let steep for 5 minutes.
3. Strain tea. Stir in stevia, if using. Serve.

BONUS RECIPES

Cheesy Keto Quiche + Apple Pie Smoothie

Ingredients:

For the Crust

- 1 cup almond flour
- 2/3 cup macadamia nuts, roasted
- 2 egg whites
- ½ tsp. sea salt
- ¼ cup and 1 Tbsp. extra virgin olive oil
- Nonstick cooking spray

For the Filling:

- 6 eggs
- 1 cup heavy cream
- ½ cup cheddar cheese
- Pinch of sea salt, to taste

Directions:

1. Preheat the oven to 350 degrees F. Lightly grease a pie pan with nonstick cooking spray. Set aside.
2. The crust is best prepared a day ahead. To do so, put together almond flour, macadamia nuts, egg whites, salt, and olive oil in a bowl. Mix until it turns into a dough.
3. Transfer to the pie pan. Spread it out. Place in the freezer for 10 minutes to set. Then, place in the oven and bake for 25 minutes.

4. Transfer to a cooling rack to cool. Cover and refrigerate until the quiche ready to cook.
5. To make the quiche filling, mix eggs, heavy cream, and cheese in a bowl. Season with salt. Mix well.
6. Pour mixture into the pie crust. Place inside the oven and bake for 25 minutes, or until the quiche is just set.
7. Place quiche on a cooling rack to cool for 10 minutes. Slice and serve.

Apple Pie Smoothie

Ingredients:

- 2 apples, quartered
- 1 tsp. cashew nuts, toasted
- 2 tsp. raisins
- Dash of nutmeg powder
- Dash of cinnamon powder, reserve some for garnish
- 1 cup crushed ice
- ½ tsp. liquid stevia, optional

Directions:

1. Place apple, cashew nuts, raisins, nutmeg powder, cinnamon powder, ice, and stevia in a blender.
2. Process until smooth. Divide into glasses. Serve.

Spinach and Ricotta Muffins + Black Currant and Lime Infusion

Ingredients:

- Nonstick cooking spray
- 10 oz. baby spinach
- 2 eggs
- ½ cup plain Greek yogurt
- 1 lb. ricotta cheese
- 2 oz. pine nuts, toasted, chopped
- 1 cup Parmesan cheese, grated
- Pinch of sea salt
- Pinch of ground black pepper, to taste

Directions:

1. Preheat the oven to 350 degrees F. Lightly grease a cup muffin tin with cooking spray. Set aside.
2. Pour just the right amount of water into the saucepan. Bring to a boil. Add in baby spinach. Blanch for 30 minutes. Drain. Set aside.
3. Chop spinach finely and then place on a bowl. Add in eggs, yogurt, ricotta cheese, pine nuts, and Parmesan cheese. Season with salt and pepper. Mix.
4. Divide mixture among muffin cups. Place inside the oven and bake for 30 minutes.
5. Place on a cooling rack and cool slightly. Serve.

Black Currant and Lime Infusion

Ingredients:

- 1 cup black currants
- 1 lime, quartered, pips removed
- 2 cups boiled water
- ¼ tsp. liquid stevia, optional

Directions:

1. Place black currants, lime, and boiled water in a tea infuser.
2. Let steep for 5 minutes.
3. Strain tea. Stir in stevia, if using. Serve.

Blueberry Scones + Grapefruit-Strawberry Smoothie

Ingredients:

- 3 eggs, beaten
- 2 tsp. baking powder
- 1 ½ cups almond flour
- ½ cup stevia
- 2 tsp. pure vanilla extract
- ¾ cup fresh or frozen raspberries

Directions:

1. Preheat the oven to 375 degrees F. Line a baking sheet with baking paper. Set aside.
2. Meanwhile, whisk in eggs, baking powder, almond flour, stevia, and vanilla extract in a mixing bowl.
3. Fold in raspberries. Stir until well combined.
4. Scoop batter onto the baking sheet. Place inside the oven and bake for 15 minutes, or until golden brown.
5. Transfer scones to a cooling rack. Let cool for 10 minutes. Serve.

Grapefruit-Strawberry Smoothie

Ingredients:

- 1 ripe grapefruit, pulp only, shredded
- 4 fresh strawberries, quartered
- 2 overripe bananas, chopped
- 1 cup shaved ice
- 2 tsp. liquid stevia, optional

Directions:

1. Place ripe grapefruit, strawberries, bananas, ice, and liquid stevia into the blender.
2. Process until smooth. Serve.

Keto Mini Waffles + Apple and Citrus Smoothie

Ingredients:

- 2 eggs
- 4 Tbsp. sour cream
- 2 Tbsp. grass-fed butter, melted
- 2 tsp. apple cider vinegar
- 4 tsp. arrowroot flour
- ½ cup almond flour
- ¼ tsp. baking powder
- ¼ tsp. baking soda
- 1 ½ tsp. stevia
- 1/8 tsp. xanthan gum
- 1/8 tsp. sea salt

Directions:

1. Preheat a mini-waffle iron on low.
2. Meanwhile, mix egg, sour cream, butter, and vinegar in a bowl. Mix well.
3. Sift arrowroot flour, almond flour, baking powder, baking soda, stevia, and xanthan gum into the sour cream and egg mixture. Gently stir until smooth.
4. Once waffle iron is hot, cook batter until firm.
5. Transfer to a tray. Serve warm.

Apple and Citrus Smoothie

Ingredients:

- 1 apple, quartered
- 1 cup ripe papaya, cubed
- 1 sweet orange, freshly juiced
- 1 cup frozen sweet grapes, halved
- 1 grapefruit, pulp only
- 1 cup crushed ice
- ½ tsp. liquid stevia, optional

Directions:

1. Place apple, papaya, sweet orange, sweet grapes, grapefruit, crushed ice, and stevia in a blender.
2. Process until smooth. Divide into portions. Serve.

Dates and Oats Bars + Apples and Carrots Infusion

Ingredients:

- 2 1/4 cups oats quick, cooking
- 2 cups whole wheat pastry flour
- 1 1/2 cups nut milk, unsweetened
- 1 1/2 cups applesauce, unsweetened
- 3/4 cup pureed dates
- 3/4 tsp sea salt
- 3 tsp baking powder
- 1 1/2 tsp ground cinnamon
- 3/4 cup organic peanut butter
- 1/3 cup pure maple syrup
- 1 1/2 tsp pure vanilla extract

Directions:

1. Preheat the oven to 350 degrees F. Line a baking dish with baking paper. Set aside.
2. Meanwhile, combine baking powder, whole wheat pastry flour, oats, cinnamon, salt in a mixing bowl.
3. In a separate bowl, mix pureed dates, nut milk, applesauce, peanut butter, and vanilla extract. Fold wet ingredients into the dry ingredients. Stir until just combined.
4. Pour batter into the baking dish. Pack firmly using a spatula.
5. Place inside the oven and bake for 25 minutes, or until a toothpick comes out clean.
6. Set on a cooling rack before slicing. Serve.

Apples and Carrots Infusion

Ingredients:

- 1 green apple, sliced into small wedges
- 1 red apple, sliced into small wedges
- 1 carrot, sliced into thin half-moons
- 1 cinnamon bark, whole
- 1 lemon, sliced into small wedges, remove pips
- 1 cup ice cubes
- 4 cups water
- 1 tsp. green stevia, optional

Directions:

1. Place green and red apples, carrot, cinnamon bark, lemon, ice cubes, water, and stevia into a glass pitcher.
2. Stir whilst bruising apples and lemons using a wooden spoon.
3. Place inside the fridge to chill for 2 hours before serving. Discard cinnamon stick
4. To serve, pour into tall glasses.

Fruity Coconut Jelly

Ingredients:

Coconut jelly

- 1 pouch unflavored gelatin
- 2 cups coconut milk, unsweetened
- 2 cups water
- 1/2 tsp. stevia
- 1 pandan leaf, whole
- Coconut oil, for greasing

Fruit salad

- ½ cup avocado, diced
- 1 pear, diced
- 1 cup young coconut meat, cubed
- 2 Tbsp. coconut flakes, toasted

Directions:

1. Lightly grease a glass baking dish with coconut oil.
2. Combine unflavored gelatin, coconut milk, water, stevia, pandan leaf in saucepan. Stir until gelatin dissolves.
3. Allow mixture to simmer while stirring continuously. Once done, turn off the heat. Discard pandan leaf.
4. Pour gelatin into the baking dish. Let cool at room temperature. Seal with saran wrap. Place inside the fridge to chill before slicing into cubes.
5. For the fruit salad, place avocado, pear, and coconut meat into a salad bowl. Add in sliced gelatin. Toss to combine.
6. To serve, ladle equal amounts into bowls. Garnish with toasted coconut flakes.

Olives and Onions Spread

Ingredients:

- 2 slices vegan bread, toasted
- 2 garlic cloves, peeled

Vegetable spread

- 1 green olive in brine, sliced thinly
- 1 black olive in oil, sliced thinly
- ⅛ cup shallot, minced
- 1 roasted red pepper in oil, julienned
- ¼ cup cucumber, julienned
- 1 tsp. apple cider vinegar
- Pinch of sea salt
- Pinch of black pepper

- ⅛ tsp. extra virgin olive oil. For drizzling

Directions:

1. Preheat the oven toaster. Rub garlic cloves on toasted bread.
2. Meanwhile, combine green olive in brine, black olive in oil, shallot, roasted red pepper in oil, cucumber, apple cider vinegar, salt, and black pepper in a bowl. Adjust taste if needed.
3. Spread on bread slices. Drizzle in olive oil. Serve.

Mushroom Crisp

Ingredients:

- 1 lb. fresh shiitake mushrooms, sliced into ¼-inch slivers
- Coconut oil, melted, for drizzling
- Pinch of sea salt
- Pinch of black pepper

Directions:

1. Preheat the oven to 300°F. Line a baking sheet with parchment paper.
2. Meanwhile, place shiitake mushrooms into a bowl. Drizzle in coconut oil.
3. Layer mushrooms on a baking sheet. Season with salt and pepper.
4. Place inside the oven and bake for 45 minutes, or until the mushrooms turn golden brown. Flip once.
5. Remove from heat. Cool slightly before serving.

CONCLUSION

Thank you again for downloading this book, ""*Vegetarian Ketogenic Diets - Healthy & Tasty Vegetarian Keto Recipes to Help Ease You into a Healthier Lifestyle & Mindset*"

I hope this book has given you a better understanding both of the Vegetarian and Ketogenic diet, and how they work. These recipes will help you jumpstart safely on said diet on your way to a healthier and slimmer physique.

The next step is to try making your own recipes and enjoy the many benefits of placing the body in ketosis. These recipes will surely make your meal planning a lot easier.

Finally, if you enjoyed this book, then I'd like to ask you for a favor, would you be kind enough to leave a review for this book on Amazon? It'd be greatly appreciated!

Thank you and good luck!